COOKIES FOR SANTA

52 KID-FRIENDLY HOLIDAY BAKING RECIPES

BY PIA IMPERIAL

ILLUSTRATED BY Risa Rodil

Grosset & Dunlap

GROSSET & DUNLAP
An imprint of Penguin Random House LLC, New York

First published in the United States of America by Grosset & Dunlap,
an imprint of Penguin Random House LLC, New York, 2023

Text copyright © 2023 by Rocco Romano
Illustrations copyright © 2023 by Risa Rodil

Visit us online at penguinrandomhouse.com.

Library of Congress Cataloging-in-Publication Data is available.

Manufactured in China

ISBN 9780593750940   10 9 8 7 6 5 4 3 2 1 TOPL

Design by Lynn Portnoff

Table of Contents

Equipment You'll Need............................... 4

Tips and Safety in the Kitchen 7

Holiday Cookies 9

Cookie Bars, Barks, and Sweet and Savory Snacks.... 28

Festive Breads, Cakes, and Desserts 49

Breakfast Bites and No-Bake Treats 63

Dietary Restriction Options 79

Conversion Tables 80

Equipment You'll Need

Here is some basic baking equipment
that you will need in the kitchen:

1. Measuring cups and spoons: for accurately measuring ingredients in recipes

2. Mixing bowls: for mixing ingredients and making doughs

3. Whisk: for whisking dry ingredients, beating eggs, and mixing liquids

4. Spatula: for scraping down bowls and pans, as well as for mixing ingredients

5. Rolling pin: for rolling out doughs, such as pie crusts and cookie dough

6. Wire rack: for cooling baked goods and preventing them from becoming soggy

7. Oven mitts or pot holders: to protect your hands when handling hot baking pans

8. Electric mixer: While not strictly necessary, an electric mixer can make mixing and beating ingredients much easier.

9. Pastry bags and tips: for decorating cakes and cupcakes. (See page 13 for a way to make your own pastry bag using common household materials.)

10. Kitchen scale: for measuring ingredients by weight, which can be more accurate than using measuring cups and spoons

11. Baking sheets and pans:
    - 8-inch round cake pan: for making layer cakes, coffee cakes, and other desserts
    - 9×13-inch baking pan: for making sheet cakes, brownies, and casseroles
    - 8-inch square baking pan: for making brownies, bars, and small casseroles
    - Springform pan: for making cheesecakes and other delicate cakes
    - Loaf pan: for making breads, meatloaf, and pound cakes
    - Muffin pan: for making muffins, cupcakes, and small cakes
    - Baking sheet: for baking cookies, biscuits, and other baked goods

12. Parchment paper: for lining baking sheets so baked goods don't stick. (Warning: Wax paper and parchment paper are not the same thing. Do not use wax paper in the oven!)

13. Cookie cutters: for cutting out shapes of your favorite cookies

Essential Items for Stocking a Baking Pantry

Leavening agents: baking powder, baking soda, cream of tartar

Sugars: granulated (white), brown (light and dark), powdered (confectioners')

Other sweeteners: honey, molasses, maple syrup, agave

Extracts: vanilla, anise, almond, peppermint

Spices: cinnamon, nutmeg, ginger, allspice, cloves

Dried fruit: cranberries, raisins, dates, coconut flakes

Nuts, legumes, and seeds: walnuts, pecans, pistachios, cashews, almonds, peanuts, pepitas

Other essentials: all-purpose flour, cooking spray, kosher salt, unsweetened cocoa powder, chocolate chips, old-fashioned rolled oats, peanut butter (and/or other nut or seed butters), jams and other fruit preserves, food coloring, sprinkles

Note: This is not an exhaustive list. These are just some of the items you'll need to stock a well-rounded pantry.

Tips and Safety in the Kitchen

1. Ask an adult for permission before cooking in the kitchen.

2. Make sure to always have an adult supervising all baking preparation in the kitchen. And only allow adults to use and operate the oven, for extra safety and precaution.

3. Wash your hands thoroughly before, during, and after baking—especially when handling raw ingredients like eggs!

4. Don't let too many dirty dishes, pots, and utensils pile up in the sink and on the counter. Clean them as you go!

5. Use a pot holder, towel, or oven-safe mitts to handle and carry hot items.

6. Do not consume any raw doughs with flour or eggs that have not been baked.

7. Have fun and enjoy your treats!

And remember that the recipes in this book are designed for the home kitchen. Each oven and microwave functions differently, so make sure to regularly check the temperature and adjust your baking as needed.

Holiday Cookies

Gingerbread Cookies 10
Easy Homemade Icing 12
Sugar Cookies 14
No-Bake Chocolate Sandwich Cookie Truffles 16
Thumbprint Cookies 18
Shortbread Cookies 20
Chocolate Crinkle Cookies 22
Snickerdoodles 24
Gluten-Free, Dairy-Free Sugar Cookies 26

Gingerbread Cookies

FOLLOW THIS SIMPLE RECIPE FOR CLASSIC GINGERBREAD COOKIES—PERFECT FOR ANY HOLIDAY CELEBRATION!

Ingredients:

3 cups all-purpose flour

1½ teaspoons ground ginger

1 teaspoon ground cinnamon

½ teaspoon ground cloves

½ teaspoon baking soda

¼ teaspoon salt

¾ cup unsalted butter, room temperature

¾ cup dark brown sugar

1 large egg

½ cup molasses

Instructions:

1. Preheat your oven to 350°F and line a baking sheet with parchment paper.

2. In a mixing bowl, whisk together the flour, ginger, cinnamon, cloves, baking soda, and salt until well combined.

3. In a separate bowl, cream together the butter and brown sugar until light and fluffy.

4. Add the egg and molasses to the wet mixture and mix until well combined.

5. Gradually mix in the dry ingredients until a soft dough forms.

6. Divide the dough in half and flatten each half into a disk.

7. Place each disk of dough between two sheets of parchment paper and roll out to about ¼-inch thickness.

8. Use cookie cutters to cut out the desired shapes and transfer them to the prepared baking sheet.

9. Bake the cookies for 10 to 12 minutes, or until the edges are set.

10. Allow the cookies to cool on the baking sheet for a few minutes before transferring them to a wire rack to cool completely.

11. Decorate the cooled cookies with easy homemade icing (see page 12 for recipe), if desired.

Get Creative!

- Use cookie cutters in the shape of gingerbread people for a fun and festive display.

- Add chopped candied ginger to the dough for an extra kick of ginger zing!

Easy Homemade Icing

HERE IS A SIMPLE RECIPE FOR A BASIC HOMEMADE ICING THAT CAN BE USED FOR CAKES, COOKIES, AND OTHER BAKED GOODS.

Ingredients:

2 cups powdered sugar

2 to 3 tablespoons milk

1 teaspoon vanilla extract (optional)

Instructions:

1. In a mixing bowl, whisk together the powdered sugar and milk until smooth.

2. If the icing is too thick, add more milk, a tablespoon at a time, or if it's too thin, add more powdered sugar.

3. If desired, add the vanilla extract and stir until well combined.

4. Use a spatula or a pastry bag to spread or pipe the icing onto your baked goods.

5. Allow the icing to set before serving.

Get Creative!

- Add 1 teaspoon of unsweetened cocoa powder for a chocolate icing.

- Add a few drops of your favorite food coloring to give your icing a festive holiday touch!

Quick Tips!

- Place 1 teaspoon of icing on the center of your cookie and use a spatula (or the back of a spoon) and spread the icing in a circular motion to evenly coat your cookie.

- To cleanly decorate your cookies, make your own pastry bag! Add the icing to a large plastic sandwich bag (preferably one with a locking seal). Press the icing into one corner of the bag and cut off just the tip of the bag's corner.

Sugar Cookies

A CLASSIC HOLIDAY COOKIE, PERFECT FOR ITS SIMPLICITY!

Ingredients:

2¾ cups all-purpose flour

1 teaspoon baking soda

½ teaspoon baking powder

1 cup unsalted butter, softened

1½ cups granulated sugar, plus ¼ cup (for rolling the dough)

1 large egg

1 teaspoon vanilla extract

Instructions:

1. Preheat your oven to 375°F and line a baking sheet with parchment paper.

2. In a medium bowl, whisk together the flour, baking soda, and baking powder.

3. In a large mixing bowl, beat the butter and 1½ cups of sugar until light and fluffy.

4. Add the egg and vanilla extract and beat until well combined.

5. Gradually add the dry ingredients to the wet mixture, mixing until just combined.

6. Shape the dough into 1½-inch balls and roll them in the remaining ¼ cup of sugar.

7. Place the dough balls on the prepared baking sheet and flatten them slightly with the bottom of a glass or fork.

8. Bake for 8 to 10 minutes or until the edges are lightly golden brown.

9. Allow the cookies to cool on the baking sheet for a few minutes before transferring them to a wire rack to cool completely.

Get Creative!

- Add your favorite holiday sprinkles or bite-size chocolate candies by pressing them lightly into each dough ball before baking.

- Top with your favorite icing (see page 12 for recipe) for a bonus festive treat!

No-Bake Chocolate Sandwich Cookie Truffles

A DECADENT HOLIDAY TREAT—NO BAKING REQUIRED!

Ingredients:

1 package (about 36 cookies) chocolate sandwich cookies

8 ounces cream cheese, softened

12 ounces semisweet chocolate chips

1 tablespoon unsalted butter

Instructions:

1. Crush the cookies into fine crumbs using a food processor or a plastic bag and a rolling pin.

2. In a mixing bowl, blend the cream cheese and cookie crumbs until well combined.

3. Roll the mixture into balls (about 1 inch in diameter) and place them on a parchment-lined baking sheet.

4. Refrigerate the balls for at least 30 minutes, or until firm.

5. In a microwave-safe bowl, melt the chocolate chips and butter in the microwave in 30-second intervals, stirring between each interval until smooth.

6. Using a fork, dip each cookie ball into the melted chocolate and tap off any excess.

7. Place the truffles back on the parchment-lined baking sheet and chill in the refrigerator until the chocolate is set.

Get Creative!

- Drizzle melted white chocolate over the truffles.

- Roll the truffles in chopped nuts or coconut before dipping them in chocolate for added holiday crunch!

- Use different flavors of chocolate sandwich cookies (like mint or peanut butter) for a unique twist on this classic recipe.

Thumbprint Cookies

FOLLOW THIS SIMPLE AND DELICIOUS RECIPE FOR CLASSIC THUMBPRINT COOKIES!

Ingredients:

- 1 cup unsalted butter, room temperature
- ½ cup granulated sugar
- 2 large egg yolks
- 1 teaspoon vanilla extract
- 2 cups all-purpose flour
- ½ teaspoon salt
- ½ cup jam or preserves (flavor of your choice)

Instructions:

1. Preheat your oven to 350°F and line a baking sheet with parchment paper.

2. In a large mixing bowl, cream together the butter and sugar until light and fluffy.

3. Add the egg yolks and vanilla extract and mix until combined.

4. In a separate bowl, whisk together the flour and salt.

5. Gradually add the dry ingredients to the wet mixture, mixing until just combined.

6. Using a cookie scoop or spoon, form the dough into 1-inch balls and place them on the prepared baking sheet.

7. Use your thumb or the back of a spoon to make an indentation in the center of each cookie.

8. Fill each indentation with a small spoonful of jam or preserves.

9. Bake for 12 to 15 minutes or until the edges are lightly golden.

10. Allow the cookies to cool on the baking sheet for a few minutes before transferring them to a wire rack to cool completely.

Get Creative!

- Roll the dough balls in chopped nuts or shredded coconut before making the indentation for added texture and flavor.

- Use different flavors of jam or preserves to create a variety of thumbprint cookies.

- Drizzle melted chocolate over the cooled cookies for a decadent twist.

Shortbread Cookies

HERE'S AN EASY RECIPE FOR CLASSIC AND BUTTERY SHORTBREAD COOKIES!

Ingredients:

1 cup unsalted butter, room temperature

½ cup granulated sugar

¼ teaspoon salt

1 teaspoon vanilla extract

2½ cups all-purpose flour

Instructions:

1. Preheat your oven to 350°F and line a baking sheet with parchment paper.

2. In a large mixing bowl, cream together the butter, sugar, and salt until light and fluffy.

3. Add the vanilla extract and mix until combined.

4. Gradually add the flour to the wet mixture, mixing until just combined.

5. Knead the dough a few times with your hands until it comes together in a smooth ball.

6. Roll out the dough on a lightly floured surface to about ¼-inch thickness.

7. Cut the dough into your desired shape (squares, circles, or wedges are traditional for shortbread).

8. Place the cookies on the prepared baking sheet, spacing them about 1 inch apart.

9. Prick each cookie all over with a fork to create little holes (this will help prevent the cookies from puffing up).

10. Bake for 12 to 15 minutes or until the edges are lightly golden.

11. Allow the cookies to cool on the baking sheet for a few minutes before transferring them to a wire rack to cool completely.

Get Creative!

- Add finely chopped nuts or citrus zest to the dough for extra flavor and crunch.

- Sprinkle the cookies with coarse sugar or a dusting of cinnamon before baking for a bonus holiday treat!

Chocolate Crinkle Cookies

A CROWD-PLEASER CLASSIC—WITH CHOCOLATE!

Ingredients:

1 cup all-purpose flour

½ cup unsweetened cocoa powder

1 teaspoon baking powder

¼ teaspoon salt

½ cup unsalted butter, room temperature

1 cup granulated sugar

2 large eggs

1 teaspoon vanilla extract

½ cup powdered sugar

Instructions:

1. In a medium bowl, whisk together the flour, cocoa powder, baking powder, and salt until combined.

2. In a large mixing bowl, cream together the butter and granulated sugar until light and fluffy.

3. Add the eggs and vanilla extract and mix until combined.

4. Gradually add the dry ingredients to the wet mixture, mixing until just combined.

5. Cover the dough with plastic wrap and refrigerate for at least 1 hour (or up to 24 hours).

6. Preheat your oven to 350°F and line a baking sheet with parchment paper.

7. Place the powdered sugar in a shallow bowl.

8. Roll the chilled dough into 1-inch balls and coat each one in the powdered sugar, making sure it's completely covered.

9. Place the cookies on the prepared baking sheet, spacing them about 2 inches apart.

10. Bake for 12 to 15 minutes or until the edges are set and the tops are cracked.

11. Allow the cookies to cool on the baking sheet for a few minutes before transferring them to a wire rack to cool completely.

Get Creative!

- Add a pinch of ground cinnamon for a bonus holiday kick!
- Add chocolate chips or chopped nuts to the dough for extra crunch and flavor.

Snickerdoodles

HERE IS A CLASSIC RECIPE FOR SNICKERDOODLE COOKIES THAT ARE SOFT, CHEWY, AND COATED IN CINNAMON SUGAR.

Ingredients:

1 cup unsalted butter, room temperature

1½ cups granulated sugar, plus ¼ cup (for rolling the dough)

2 large eggs

2¾ cups all-purpose flour

2 teaspoons cream of tartar

1 teaspoon baking soda

½ teaspoon salt

2 teaspoons ground cinnamon

Instructions:

1. Preheat your oven to 350°F and line a baking sheet with parchment paper.

2. In a large mixing bowl, cream together the butter and 1½ cups of sugar until light and fluffy.

3. Beat in the eggs one at a time, mixing well after each addition.

4. In a separate bowl, whisk together the flour, cream of tartar, baking soda, and salt.

5. Gradually add the dry ingredients to the wet mixture, mixing until just combined.

6. In a small bowl, mix the cinnamon and remaining ¼ cup of sugar.

7. Using a cookie scoop or spoon, form the dough into 1½-inch balls and roll each one in the cinnamon-sugar mixture until coated.

8. Place the cookies on the prepared baking sheet, spacing them about 2 inches apart.

9. Bake for 10 to 12 minutes or until the edges are lightly golden.

10. Allow the cookies to cool on the baking sheet for a few minutes before transferring them to a wire rack to cool completely.

Get Creative!

- Add a pinch of ground nutmeg or allspice to the cinnamon-sugar mixture for even more holiday spice.

- Use a mixture of granulated sugar and brown sugar for an even deeper flavor.

Gluten-Free, Dairy-Free Sugar Cookies

Ingredients:

1 cup gluten-free flour blend

½ teaspoon baking powder

¼ teaspoon salt

⅓ cup coconut oil, melted

⅓ cup maple syrup

1 egg

1 teaspoon vanilla extract

Instructions:

1. Preheat your oven to 350°F and line a baking sheet with parchment paper.

2. In a medium bowl, whisk together the flour, baking powder, and salt.

3. In a separate bowl, whisk together the coconut oil, maple syrup, egg, and vanilla extract.

4. Add the dry ingredients to the wet mixture and mix until a smooth dough forms.

5. Roll out the dough on a floured surface to ¼-inch thickness.

6. Use cookie cutters to cut out the desired shapes and place them on the prepared baking sheet.

7. Bake for 8 to 10 minutes or until the edges are lightly browned.

8. Let the cookies cool on the baking sheet for a few minutes before transferring them to a wire rack to cool completely.

Get Creative!

- Decorate your cookies with icing (see page 12 for recipe) or sprinkles for an extra holiday touch!

Cookie Bars, Barks, and Sweet and Savory Snacks

Cookie Bars 30

Chocolate Chip Cookie 31
Chocolate Mint 33
Maple Pecan 33
Chocolate Cherry Chip 33
Peppermint Cranberry Chip 33
Sugar Cookie 34
Ginger Molasses 35
Christmas Sprinkle 35
Classic Brownie 36
Peanut Butter Cup Brownie 37

Christmas Mint Brownie 37
No-Bake Trail Mix Bars 38

Barks 40

White Chocolate Christmas 41
Peppermint Pretzel 41
Cookies and Cream 41
Granola 42
Peanut Butter 42
Macadamia Nut and Lime Zest 42
Cranberry, Pistachio, and Sea Salt 42
Cherry, Pecans, and Sea Salt 43
Roasted Almonds and Flaky Coconut 43
Chocolate-Covered Peanuts and Raisins 43
Chocolate Hazelnut 43

Sweet and Savory Snacks 44

Christmas Crunch Popcorn 45
Chocolate-Dipped Pretzel Rods 46
Easy Trail Mix 46

Cookie Bars

Cookie Bar Basics

Follow these four easy steps to
create simple cookie bars:

1. Preheat your oven to 350°F.

2. Line an 8-inch square baking pan with aluminum foil or
   parchment paper and coat with cooking spray or melted
   butter.

3. Prepare your batter or dough. Spread into the pan.

4. Bake as directed. Transfer to a rack and let cool.

Chocolate Chip Cookie

Ingredients:

3 cups all-purpose flour

1 teaspoon baking soda

1 tablespoon cornstarch

1 teaspoon salt

1 cup unsalted butter, melted

$\frac{2}{3}$ cup granulated sugar

1 cup light brown sugar

2 eggs, room temperature

1 tablespoon vanilla extract

2 cups semisweet chocolate chips

Instructions:

1. Preheat your oven to 350°F and line an 8-inch square baking pan with aluminum foil or parchment paper and coat with cooking spray or melted butter.

2. Combine the flour, baking soda, cornstarch, and salt in a medium bowl.

3. In a separate bowl, add the butter.

4. Add the granulated sugar and brown sugar to the butter and mix until a thick slurry forms.

5. Add the eggs and vanilla extract to the butter mixture and mix until well combined. Pour the flour mixture into the wet mixture and combine. Then stir in the chocolate chips. Transfer the batter to the pan and spread evenly.

6. Bake for 35 minutes or until the edges are set. To check doneness, quickly insert a toothpick into the center. If it comes out clean, the cookie bars are done.

7. Let cool on a wire rack before removing and cutting into 2-inch squares.

Here are some more delicious cookie bars you can make by following the Chocolate Chip Cookie bar recipe (on page 31) and making the appropriate substitutions and changes.

Chocolate Mint
Substitute crushed chocolate-mint sandwich cookies for chocolate chips.

Maple Pecan
Substitute maple syrup for brown sugar. Substitute chopped pecans for chocolate chips.

Chocolate Cherry Chip
Reduce the chocolate chips to 1 cup and add 1 cup of chopped dried cherries. Substitute almond extract for vanilla extract.

Peppermint Cranberry Chip
Reduce the chocolate chips to 1 cup and add 1 cup of chopped dried cranberries. Substitute peppermint extract for vanilla extract.

Sugar Cookie

Ingredients:

1 cup unsalted butter, melted

1½ cups granulated sugar

2 eggs, room temperature

1 tablespoon vanilla extract

2 cups all-purpose flour

¼ teaspoon salt

Instructions:

1. Preheat your oven to 350°F and line an 8-inch square baking pan with aluminum foil or parchment paper and coat with cooking spray or melted butter.

2. Add the butter to a large mixing bowl.

3. Whisk in the sugar, eggs, and vanilla extract to form a thick slurry.

4. Stir in the flour and salt.

5. Transfer the batter to the prepared pan and bake until the edges are set, about 25 minutes.

Try these holiday spins on the classic sugar cookie bar:

Ginger Molasses

Follow the Sugar Cookie bar recipe, using only ½ cup of granulated sugar and adding ½ cup each of light brown sugar and molasses. Add 1 teaspoon of ground ginger with the dry ingredients. Optional: sprinkle with chopped candied ginger before baking.

Christmas Sprinkle

Follow the Sugar Cookie bar recipe, folding ½ cup total of red, green, and white sprinkles into the batter before transferring to the prepared pan. Spread vanilla frosting over the cooled bars and top with more sprinkles.

Classic Brownie

Ingredients:

1 cup unsalted butter, melted

4 ounces semisweet chocolate, chopped

2 cups granulated sugar

4 eggs, room temperature

1½ cups all-purpose flour

⅓ cup unsweetened cocoa powder

½ teaspoon salt

Instructions:

1. Preheat your oven to 350°F and line an 8-inch square baking pan with aluminum foil or parchment paper and coat with cooking spray or melted butter.

2. In a large mixing bowl, combine the butter and chocolate. Stir in the sugar and eggs. Whisk in the flour, cocoa powder, and salt.

3. Transfer to the prepared pan and bake for 30 to 35 minutes, until a toothpick comes out clean.

4. Let cool and cut into small squares.

Try these holiday spins on the classic brownie bar!

Peanut Butter Cup Brownie

Follow the Classic Brownie bar recipe. Press 16 small chocolate peanut butter cups into the batter in the pan before baking.

Christmas Mint Brownie

Follow the Classic Brownie bar recipe. As soon as you pull the brownies from the oven, top with 16 of your favorite bite-size mint candies. Using a spatula (or a knife or the back of a spoon), spread the melted candy evenly.

No-Bake Trail Mix Bars

Ingredients:

¾ cup nut butter (peanut, almond, or walnut–the drippier the better)

1 tablespoon coconut oil

½ cup maple syrup or honey

2 cups grain cereal of your choice

1 cup quick oats

⅓ cup shelled hemp seeds

⅓ cup raisins or other dried fruit

⅓ cup chopped/sliced almonds or other nuts

⅛ teaspoon sea salt

Instructions:

1. Line an 8-inch square pan with parchment paper.

2. Microwave the nut butter and coconut oil for 30 seconds in a large microwave-safe cup or bowl. Stir in the maple syrup (or honey) and allow to cool, about 2 minutes.

3. Mix the dry ingredients into the nut butter mixture. Pour the mixture into the lined pan and push the mixture down into the corners.

4. Cover and freeze for 1 hour. Cut into bars.

Barks

Chocolate Bark Basics

Follow these three easy steps to make your own homemade bark:

1. Choose a base. Melt 16 ounces of your preferred chocolate chips–bittersweet, semisweet, milk, or white–in a microwave-safe bowl for 20-second intervals, stirring after each interval. Repeat until fully melted (2 to 3 minutes).

2. Choose your toppings. Line a rimmed baking sheet with wax or parchment paper and place the toppings and fillings of your choice on the lined baking sheet.

3. Make the bark. Pour the melted chocolate over the toppings. Place the baking sheet in the refrigerator and chill until the bark hardens, about 1 hour. Break into pieces and enjoy!

Quick Tip!

Homemade bark can be stored in an airtight container at room temperature for up to two weeks.

Holiday Bark Favorites

Follow the Chocolate Bark Basics recipe (on page 40) and add the appropriate fillings and toppings for a festive holiday spin on a classic!

White Chocolate Christmas

Pour white chocolate over red and green chocolate candies and crushed peppermint sticks. Top with holiday sprinkles!

Peppermint Pretzel

Pour milk chocolate over crushed peppermint sticks and mini pretzels.

Cookies and Cream

Pour white chocolate over crushed chocolate sandwich cookies and chocolate chips.

Granola

Pour semisweet chocolate over your favorite granola! See page 66 for some holiday granola recipes.

Peanut Butter

Place 12 dollops of peanut butter (or any nut butter) evenly on the lined baking sheet. Pour milk chocolate over the dollops and use a spatula (or the back of a knife) to spread evenly.

Holiday Bark Favorites . . . with Nuts!

Follow the Chocolate Bark Basics recipe (on page 40) and add the appropriate fillings and toppings for a festive holiday spin on a classic!

Macadamia Nut and Lime Zest

Pour white chocolate onto the lined baking sheet. Add macadamia nuts evenly and top with the zest of 1 lime.

Cranberry, Pistachio, and Sea Salt

Pour white chocolate onto the lined baking sheet. Add dried

cranberries and pistachios evenly and top with a few pinches of sea salt.

Cherry, Pecans, and Sea Salt

Pour semisweet chocolate onto the lined baking sheet. Add dried cherries and pecans and top with a few pinches of sea salt.

Roasted Almonds and Flaky Coconut

Pour milk chocolate over the roasted almonds. Top with coconut flakes (about 2 to 3 tablespoons, depending on how much you like!).

Chocolate-Covered Peanuts and Raisins

Pour white chocolate onto the lined baking sheet. Add chocolate-covered peanuts (or another covered nut) and raisins.

Chocolate Hazelnut

Add 12 dollops of chocolate hazelnut spread to the lined baking sheet. Pour semisweet or milk chocolate over the dollops and use a spatula (or the back of a knife) to spread evenly. Top with hazelnuts.

Sweet and Savory Snacks

CRAVING SOMETHING SWEET AND SAVORY? HERE ARE SOME FUN AND EASY SNACKS FOR THE WHOLE FAMILY!

Christmas Crunch Popcorn

Follow these three easy steps for delicious sweet and savory popcorn:

1. Prepare a bag or two of your favorite popcorn. Place the popcorn on a baking sheet lined with wax paper.

2. Add mini pretzels, your favorite holiday bark, or red and green candy melts (or all three!) to the lined baking sheet.

3. Melt your preferred chocolate in a microwave-safe bowl. Pour chocolate over popcorn mix. Top with holiday sprinkles and let chocolate cool.

Chocolate-Dipped Pretzel Rods

Follow these three easy steps for a sweet and savory pretzel treat:

1. Melt your preferred chocolate in a microwave-safe bowl.

2. Dip half of a pretzel rod into the chocolate.

3. While still warm, roll the chocolate-covered pretzel into your favorite crushed candy or holiday sprinkles!

Easy Trail Mix

To make your own homemade trail mix, combine equal parts of your favorite nuts and seeds, dried fruit, and grain.

Here are some fun suggestions:

Nuts, legumes, and seeds: **peanuts, almonds, walnuts, cashews, pistachios, hazelnuts, shelled hemp seeds, flaxseed**

Dried fruit: **mango, cranberries, cherries, blueberries, apricots, raisins**

Grain: **quick or old-fashioned rolled oats, cereal, pretzels, puffed quinoa**

Quick Tip!

Store your trail mix in an airtight container for up to a month.

Get Creative!

- Add your favorite holiday candies for a festive treat: red and green chocolate candies, toffee, or your favorite bark (see page 41 for a list of barks).

Festive Breads, Cakes, and Desserts

Easy Homemade Banana Bread 50
5-Minute Mug Cakes 52
Apple Brown Betty 54
Festive Bread Pudding 56
No-Bake Peppermint Cheesecake 58
Holiday Marshmallow Crispy Rice Treats 60

Easy Homemade Banana Bread

A CLASSIC, SIMPLE RECIPE—PERFECT FOR WHEN YOU HAVE OVERRIPE BANANAS!

Ingredients:

3 ripe bananas, mashed

$\frac{1}{3}$ cup unsalted butter, melted

1 teaspoon baking soda

Pinch of salt

$\frac{3}{4}$ cup granulated sugar

1 large egg, beaten

1 teaspoon vanilla extract

$1\frac{1}{2}$ cups all-purpose flour

Instructions:

1. Preheat your oven to 350°F and grease a 9×5-inch loaf pan.

2. In a mixing bowl, combine the bananas and butter.

3. Add in the baking soda and salt and stir.

4. Mix in the sugar, egg, and vanilla extract.

5. Stir in the flour until just combined. Do not overmix.

6. Pour the batter into the prepared loaf pan.

7. Bake for 50 to 60 minutes, or until a toothpick inserted into the center of the bread comes out clean.

8. Allow the bread to cool in the pan for 10 minutes before transferring to a wire rack to cool completely.

Get Creative!

- Once cooled, top with a dollop of your favorite homemade whipped cream (see page 74 for recipe) and sprinkles for a bonus holiday treat!

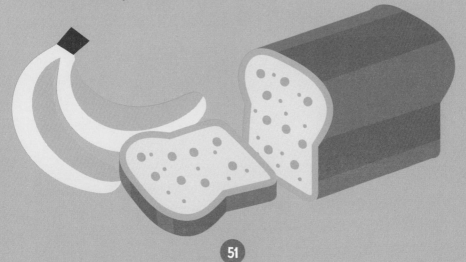

5-Minute Mug Cakes

THESE QUICK AND EASY MUG CAKES ARE PERFECT FOR ANY HOLIDAY OR CELEBRATION!

Vanilla Mug Cake

Ingredients:

4 tablespoons all-purpose flour

2 tablespoons granulated sugar

¼ teaspoon baking powder

⅛ teaspoon salt

3 tablespoons milk

1 tablespoon vegetable oil

¼ teaspoon vanilla extract

Instructions:

1. In a microwave-safe mug, whisk together the flour, sugar, baking powder, and salt until well combined.

2. Add in the milk, vegetable oil, and vanilla extract, and whisk until the batter is smooth and free of lumps.

3. Microwave the mug cake on high for 1 minute and 30 seconds. (Microwave times may vary depending on the wattage of your microwave. You may need to adjust the cooking time accordingly.)

4. Carefully remove the mug from the microwave (it will be hot!), and let it cool for a few minutes before digging in.

Get Creative!

- After microwaving, top your mug cake with one of these holiday toppings: chocolate chips, crushed peppermint sticks, or fresh berries and homemade whipped cream!

- To make a Chocolate Mug Cake, follow the recipe above but add 2 tablespoons of unsweetened cocoa powder.

Apple Brown Betty

A CRUMBLY APPLE DESSERT WITH DELICIOUS WINTER SPICES. HONEYCRISP, GALA, OR MCINTOSH APPLES WORK GREAT!

Ingredients:

4 cups peeled, sliced apples (about 4 apples)

¼ cup orange juice

¾ cup all-purpose flour

1 cup granulated sugar

¼ teaspoon ground nutmeg

½ teaspoon ground cinnamon

Pinch of salt

½ cup unsalted butter

Instructions:

1. Preheat your oven to 375°F and grease a round 8-inch pan.

2. Mound the apples in the pan and pour the orange juice over the apples.

3. In a bowl, mix the flour, sugar, nutmeg, cinnamon, and salt, and then cut in the butter until crumbly. Place flour mixture over the apples.

4. Bake for 45 minutes, until golden brown on top and the apples are tender.

Get Creative!

• Enjoy while warm with a scoop of homemade whipped cream (see page 74 for recipe) or vanilla ice cream!

Festive Bread Pudding

THE PERFECT RECIPE FOR A COZY CHRISTMAS MORNING BREAKFAST OR A WARM AND COMFORTING DESSERT AFTER A HOLIDAY DINNER. IT'S ALSO A GREAT WAY TO USE UP LEFTOVER BREAD FROM YOUR HOLIDAY FEAST!

Ingredients:

3 cups milk

1 cup heavy cream

4 eggs

½ cup granulated sugar

1 tablespoon vanilla extract

1 teaspoon ground cinnamon

¼ teaspoon ground nutmeg

¼ teaspoon salt

1 loaf of bread, cut into 1-inch cubes (brioche, challah, and Pullman are great choices!)

½ cup raisins (optional)

Instructions:

1. Preheat your oven to 350°F and grease a 9×13-inch baking dish.

2. In a large mixing bowl, whisk together the milk, heavy cream, eggs, sugar, vanilla extract, cinnamon, nutmeg, and salt until well combined.

3. Add the bread cubes and raisins (if using) to the mixing bowl and stir gently until the bread is fully coated.

4. Pour the bread mixture into the prepared baking dish and spread it out evenly.

5. Bake for 45 to 50 minutes or until the top is golden brown and the center is set.

6. Let the bread pudding cool for a few minutes before serving.

Get Creative!

• Serve warm and top with a dollop of your favorite homemade whipped cream! (See page 74 for recipe.)

No-Bake Peppermint Cheesecake

THE ULTIMATE DECADENT DESSERT THAT REQUIRES NO BAKING!

Ingredients:

- 1½ cups chocolate wafer cookies (or chocolate graham crackers), crushed
- ⅓ cup unsalted butter, melted
- 1 cup heavy cream
- 8 ounces cream cheese, softened
- 1 cup powdered sugar
- 1 teaspoon vanilla extract
- ½ teaspoon peppermint extract
- ½ cup peppermint candies (or candy canes), crushed

Instructions:

1. In a mixing bowl, combine the cookies and butter until well mixed.

2. Press the cookie mixture into the bottom of a 9-inch springform pan to form a crust. Set aside.

3. In a separate mixing bowl, whip the heavy cream until stiff peaks form. Set aside.

4. In a large mixing bowl, beat the cream cheese until smooth and creamy.

5. Gradually add the powdered sugar and continue to beat until well combined.

6. Add the vanilla extract and peppermint extract and beat until combined.

7. Fold in the whipped cream and peppermint candies.

8. Spoon the cheesecake mixture over the cookie crust and spread it out evenly.

9. Chill the cheesecake in the refrigerator for at least 2 hours, or until set.

Get Creative!

- Top with additional whipped cream and crushed peppermint candies to make it even more festive!

Holiday Marshmallow Crispy Rice Treats

Ingredients:

¼ cup unsalted butter

10 ounces (1 package) marshmallows

½ teaspoon vanilla extract

¼ teaspoon salt (optional)

6 cups crispy rice cereal

Instructions:

1. Grease a 9×13-inch baking dish with cooking spray or butter.

2. Melt the butter in a large saucepan over low heat.

3. Add the marshmallows and stir until melted and smooth.

4. Remove the pan from the heat and stir in the vanilla extract and salt (if using).

5. Stir in the cereal until well coated with the marshmallow mixture.

6. Pour the mixture into the prepared baking dish and press down firmly with a spatula or your hands to evenly distribute.

7. Allow the treats to cool and set for at least 30 minutes before cutting into squares.

Get Creative!

- Add sprinkles or colored sugar to the mixture for a fun, colorful twist.

- Stir in mini chocolate chips or chopped nuts for added texture and flavor.

- Use different flavored marshmallows–like strawberry or caramel–for a unique twist on this holiday classic!

Breakfast Bites and No-Bake Treats

Morning Muffins 64
Homemade Granola with Dried Fruit and Nuts 66
Fruit and Yogurt Parfait. 68
Baked Breakfast Oats. 70
French Toast 72
Homemade Whipped Cream 74

5 Easy No-Bake Energy Bites. . .76

Banana Nut. 78
Pumpkin Pie 78
Nut Bonanza. 78
Omega Bombs 78
4C Bites 78

Morning Muffins

Ingredients:

2 cups all-purpose flour

½ cup granulated sugar

2 teaspoons baking powder

½ teaspoon salt

½ cup unsalted butter, melted

1 cup milk

2 large eggs

1 teaspoon vanilla extract

1 cup mix-ins (blueberries, chopped nuts, and chocolate chips are classic options)

Instructions:

1. Preheat your oven to 375°F. Grease or line a 12-cup muffin tin with paper liners.

2. In a large bowl, whisk together the flour, sugar, baking powder, and salt until combined.

3. In a separate bowl, whisk together the butter, milk, eggs, and vanilla extract.

4. Add the dry ingredients to the wet mixture and stir until just combined (it's okay if there are a few lumps!).

5. Gently fold in the mix-ins (like blueberries or chocolate chips).

6. Divide the batter evenly among the muffin cups (filling each about three-quarters full).

7. Bake for 20 to 25 minutes or until a toothpick inserted into the center of a muffin comes out clean.

8. Allow the muffins to cool in the tin for a few minutes before moving them to a wire rack to cool completely.

Get Creative!

- Experiment with different mix-ins, like raspberries, chopped apples, or shredded coconut.

Homemade Granola with Dried Fruit and Nuts

SIMPLE, DELICIOUS, AND NUTRITIOUS!

Ingredients:

- 4 cups old-fashioned rolled oats
- 2 cups nuts/seeds
- ¾ teaspoon kosher salt
- ½ teaspoon ground cinnamon
- ½ cup oil (either extra-virgin olive oil or coconut oil)
- ½ cup sweetener (honey, maple syrup, or agave)
- 1 teaspoon vanilla extract
- 1 cup dried fruit

Instructions:

1. Preheat your oven to 350°F. Line a rimmed baking sheet with parchment paper.

2. Mix the rolled oats, nuts/seeds, salt, and cinnamon in a large bowl. Pour the oil, sweetener, and vanilla extract over the oat mixture and mix until well combined. Transfer the granola onto the lined baking sheet and spread into an even layer.

3. Bake until lightly golden brown (about 22 to 25 minutes). Remove from the oven and top with dried fruit. Allow for the granola to cool completely before enjoying.

Get Creative!

- Try a combination of your favorite nuts and seeds, like almonds, pecans, walnuts, or pepitas.

- Use your favorite dried fruits, like cherries, cranberries, apricots, or dates.

- Top with chocolate chips, coconut flakes, or sprinkles for a bonus holiday crunch!

Fruit and Yogurt Parfait

TO MAKE YOUR OWN HOLIDAY FRUIT AND YOGURT PARFAIT, CHOOSE YOUR FAVORITE FRUITS AND LAYER THEM IN BETWEEN THE YOGURT OF CHOICE. THICK GREEK-STYLE YOGURT IS A GREAT OPTION. TOP WITH SOME GRANOLA FOR A BONUS HEALTHY CRUNCH!

Ingredients:

½ cup yogurt

½ cup fruit of your choice

¼ cup toppings of your choice

Instructions:

1. Place half the yogurt in a mason jar or cup of your choice. Add some fruit and add the rest of the yogurt. Finish with your favorite toppings!

   Fruits: strawberry, blueberry, raspberry, blackberry, mango

   Toppings: granola, trail mix, quick and old-fashioned rolled oats, coconut flakes, flaxseed, chia seeds

Get Creative!

- To make your parfait a delicious dessert, swap in your favorite ice cream or frozen yogurt for the yogurt. Top with whipped cream and sprinkles!

Baked Breakfast Oats

AN EASY AND DELICIOUS WAY TO START YOUR MORNING!

Ingredients:

½ cup old-fashioned rolled oats

¼ cup milk of your choice (dairy, oat, almond, soy)

½ medium ripe banana

1 tablespoon pure maple syrup

1 tablespoon strawberry jam, plus a little more for topping

1 teaspoon baking powder

1 teaspoon vanilla extract

½ cup fresh strawberries, diced, plus a little more for topping

Instructions:

1. Preheat your oven to 350°F and grease a small oven-safe bowl or pan.

2. In a blender, add the rolled oats, milk, banana, maple syrup, jam, baking powder, and vanilla extract. Blend until smooth, like pancake batter. Fold the strawberries into the oat batter.

3. Pour the oat batter into the prepared bowl or pan.

4. Bake for 20 to 25 minutes, until lightly golden brown.

5. Remove from the oven and top with more strawberries and drizzle with jam.

Quick Tip!

This recipe is gluten-free and nut-free, and can be made dairy-free and vegan with the proper milk!

French Toast

A CLASSIC RECIPE—PERFECT FOR USING UP DAY-OLD BREAD!

Ingredients:

4 egg yolks, room temperature

1 cup milk

2 tablespoons granulated sugar

2 teaspoons vanilla extract

½ teaspoon ground cinnamon

Pinch of kosher salt

4 thick-cut pieces of day-old bread (brioche, challah, or Pullman work best)

4 tablespoons unsalted butter (for cooking the toast)

Instructions:

1. Add all the ingredients (except the bread and butter) to a large bowl and whisk together until fully incorporated.

2. Place the four pieces of bread onto a rimmed baking sheet or a similar container.

3. Pour the batter over the bread. Allow the bread to fully soak in the batter. Flip each piece of bread to get both sides nicely covered.

4. Working in batches, place a tablespoon of butter per slice of bread in a nonstick pan and cook over medium heat until the bread is golden brown (about 2 to 3 minutes). Flip and cook the other side.

5. To keep the toast warm while cooking the other batches, place in a 200°F oven.

Get Creative!

- Top your french toast with fresh berries and your favorite whipped cream (see recipe on page 74).

- For a bonus holiday treat, add some sprinkles or red and green chocolate candies!

Homemade Whipped Cream

THE PERFECT PAIRING FOR YOUR FAVORITE HOLIDAY COOKIES, DESSERTS, AND TREATS!

Ingredients:

1 cup heavy cream

2 tablespoons granulated sugar

1 teaspoon vanilla extract

Instructions:

1. Chill a large mixing bowl in the refrigerator for at least 15 minutes.

2. Add the heavy cream, sugar, and vanilla extract to the chilled mixing bowl.

3. Use an electric mixer to beat the mixture on medium speed until it starts to thicken.

4. Increase the speed to high and continue beating until stiff peaks form.

5. Serve immediately, or store in an airtight container in the refrigerator.

Get Creative!

- Adjust the amount of sugar to your desired sweetness.

- Add different flavors or extracts–like almond, coconut, cocoa, or maple (¼ teaspoon or to your desired liking)–to customize the whipped cream to your taste.

- For a fun pop of color, add 5 to 10 drops of your favorite holiday food coloring.

Quick Tip!

Whipped cream will last about three days in the refrigerator. To freeze, place the whipped cream into small mounds on a parchment-lined baking sheet until frozen. Remove the mounds and store in a freezer-safe container for up to three months.

5 Easy No-Bake Energy Bites

Get creative and make your own energy bites by combining 1 cup of old-fashioned rolled oats with your choice of ½ cup of nut/seed butter, 1 tablespoon of liquid, and 2 to 3 tablespoons of sweetener.

Here are some base choices:

Nut/seed butter: peanut, cashew, almond, sunflower

Liquid: any milk of your choice, water, coconut oil

Sweetener: honey, maple syrup, agave

Then, add ½ cup of any of the following (you can mix and match, too!):

Chocolate chips

White chocolate chips

Mashed fresh fruit or fruit puree

Dried fruit

Coconut flakes

Flaxseed

Shelled hemp or chia seeds

Instructions:

1. In a large mixing bowl, combine the rolled oats, nut/seed butter, liquid, and ½ cup of the add-ons.

2. Add the sweetener a little at a time to your liking.

3. Stir together until the mixture becomes sticky.

4. If the mixture is too dry, add more liquid, 1 tablespoon at a time.

5. Place the bowl in the freezer for 2 minutes.

6. Remove from the freezer and roll the oat mixture into small balls.

Get Creative!

- To make your energy bites even more festive for the holiday, make a quick mixture of ¼ cup of granulated sugar and 15 to 20 drops of food coloring.

- Make one mixture red and another green and roll half the balls in one color and half in the other.

Here are some variations with more fun add-ons to try!

Banana Nut
Mashed banana, chopped nuts, dried fruit

Pumpkin Pie
Pumpkin puree, chopped pumpkin seeds, ground cinnamon, ground cloves, ground nutmeg

Nut Bonanza
Almond slivers, chopped pecans, cashews

Omega Bombs
Chia and shelled hemp seeds, chopped walnuts, dried blueberries

4C Bites
Chocolate chips, coconut flakes, chia seeds, dried cherries

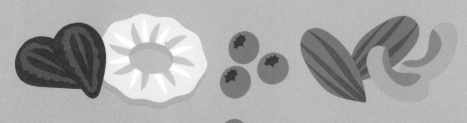

Dietary Restriction Options

- To make any recipe gluten-free, swap in Bob's Red Mill 1-to-1 baking flour (or any store-bought mixture of gluten-free flours).

- To make any recipe dairy-free, swap in your alternative milk of choice (soy, almond, oat, cashew, hemp, etc.).

- Omit nuts and nut butters as needed to make nut-free. Add equal volume of an appropriate add-in (like chocolate chips or seed butter) to maintain recipe quality.

Conversion Tables

Temperature

350°F = 180°C   375°F = 190°C   400°F = 200°C   425°F = 220°C

Other Handy Baking Conversions

- 1 cup all-purpose flour = 120 grams
- 1 cup granulated sugar = 200 grams
- 1 cup brown sugar = 220 grams
- 1 cup butter = 227 grams
- 1 cup liquid = 16 tablespoons = 8 fluid ounces
- ¼ cup = 4 tablespoons
- 1 tablespoon = 3 teaspoons = 15 milliliters
- 1 teaspoon = 5 milliliters

Eggs come in different sizes, and it's important to use the right size for your recipe when it calls for more than one.

Here are some common egg size conversions:

- 2 large eggs = 2 medium eggs = 3 small eggs
- 5 large eggs = 6 medium eggs = 7 small eggs